THIS JOURNAL
BELONGS TO

____

LIVING LIBERATED

A 21-DAY DEVOTIONAL COMPANION

Daily Truths to Reclaim Who God Says You Are

SYRENA N. WILLIAMS

Contents

How To Use This Devotional
Introduction
A Note On Liberation And Love

Day 1: Made for More 01

Day 2: Never First, Always Second 05

Day 3: Grace Over Grind 09

Day 4: Not Validated, Chosen 13

Day 5: Embracing My Divine Design 17

Day 6: Obedience Over Certainty 21

Day 7: Worth the Wait 25

Contents

Day 8: Trusting God in Transition29

Day 9: Released and Restored33

Day 10: Forgiveness Is An Act of Faith37

Day 11: The Holy Cadence of Rest41

Day 12: Chosen to Break the Pattern45

Day 13: Divinely Drafted49

Day 14: Fully Known, Fully Loved53

Day 15: No Longer Negotiating My Worth57

Day 16: The Power of a Sacred No61

Day 17: Joy Is My Rebellion65

Day 18: Grief Is Holy Too69

Day 19: Becoming Whole, Not Flawless73

Day 20: Walking in the Light77

Day 21: Living Liberated81

About Me

Other Books

How To Use This Devotional

This devotional companion is not meant to impress you, it was written to walk with you. You won't find perfection here, but you will find truth, compassion, and a clear reminder that no matter where you've been, God is still writing your story and calling you forward.

These 21 days are not a formula for quick healing. They are an invitation to slow down, listen for God's voice, and gently confront the lies, labels, and longings that may have shaped how you see yourself. Each entry offers a moment to reflect, reframe, and reclaim the freedom that is already yours in Christ.

There's no magic in the number 21; however, there is power in showing up for yourself daily. Whether you engage this devotional over consecutive days or choose to experience it another way. When you pick it up pause and linger where God speaks loudest. In whatever way you choose, trust that He will meet you where you are.

Each day includes:

- A title grounded in real experiences and transformation

- A passage of Scripture to anchor your heart

- A short reflection to encourage and challenge you

- A Prayer Starter to guide your time with God

- A journal prompt to help you process and respond

You don't need to be perfect. You don't need to have all the answers. You just need a willing heart and a few quiet moments each day.

Come as you are, God already knows, and He still chose you.

Let's begin.

Introduction

Living Liberated didn't begin with a breakthrough.

It began with a breakdown.

For years, I lived by a script I didn't write. I performed roles I never auditioned for dutiful, quiet, responsible, needed, nice. I lived beneath labels handed to me by culture, trauma, fear, and even religion. I confused people-pleasing with love. I mistook survival for strength. And I wore my pain like it was proof of my purpose.

But beneath the mask, I was tired. Tired of shrinking. Tired of striving. Tired of pretending I didn't have needs, desires, or dreams. I had spent so much of my life being who I thought I had to be that I no longer recognized who I really was.

And that's where liberation began.

Not with perfection. Not with performance.

The goal isn't to avoid falling. The goal is to learn balance.

We don't have to hide in shame from ourselves. Liberation is accepting the areas we want to grow in with self-love.

Perfection demands flawlessness. Performance demands acting.

But growth demands courage.

And courage leads to truth and change.

This devotional is about the journey to reclaim that truth. It's about letting go of the lies that told you that you were unworthy, the labels that kept you in boxes, and the longing that drove you to chase what you already had access to in God.

It's not a self-help manual.

It's a mirror.

A companion.

A collection of honest reflections, spiritual insight, and hard-earned wisdom.

It's about breaking up with the patterns, beliefs, and attachments that have held, or are still holding you hostage, and learning how to shift and rewire those cycles so you can live whole, free, and deeply loved.

If you've ever felt like you were too much or not enough, like you had to dim your light just to fit in, or as if you lost yourself trying to be what everyone else needed, you're not alone.

This is not a story of blame.

It's a story of awakening.

A story of remembering who you were before the world told you who to be.

It's an invitation: To grieve what you thought you had to become.

To confront what you were never meant to carry.

And to choose a life that's aligned with the truth of who God created you to be.

Let's walk it out together, one truth at a time.

You don't have to perform anymore.

You don't have to prove anything.

You don't have to wait to be chosen.

You already are.

A Note On Liberation And Love

Liberation is not just about escape, it's about encounter. True freedom isn't measured by how far you've run from something, but by how deeply you've rooted yourself in God's truth.

To be liberated is to walk in the freedom that Jesus Christ died and rose to give you. It's to say: I don't have to live in fear. I don't have to shrink to be accepted. I don't have to perform to be loved. I can be healed. I can be whole. I can be fully seen and fully received because God has already called me worthy.

Love is what unlocks that truth. Not the world's version of love, but the kind that starts with God. In Matthew 22:37–39, Jesus tells us to love God with all our heart, soul, and mind, then to love our neighbor as ourselves. But many of us were never taught to focus on loving ourselves before loving others. Oftentimes we skip straight to giving, fixing, and performing for others without first receiving God's love for ourselves.

You can't give what you haven't received.

God's love is not transactional. It's transformational. It heals, convicts, covers, and restores. And when you let it in, when you truly believe that God's love is for you, not just in theory, but in practice, you begin to live differently.

So this is your reminder, as you walk through these pages:

You were made to be free.

You were made to be loved.

And you were made to love, from the inside out, starting with the God who created you, redeemed you, and calls you by name.

DAY 1
Made for More

Scripture: John 10:10 (New International Version, NIV)

"The thief comes only to steal and kill and destroy; I have come that they may have life, and have it to the full."

Reflection

The enemy doesn't need a brand-new strategy; he just needs you to forget who you are. Jesus tells us plainly: "The thief comes only to steal, kill, and destroy." And for many of us, the first thing he comes to steal is our joy. Not in one big moment, but little by little through doubt, distraction, discouragement, and delay.

You were not created to merely exist. You were made to thrive. But somewhere along the way, you may have accepted less, less joy, less clarity, less freedom. Maybe you've been surviving when God designed you for overflow. Maybe you've believed that struggle is holy and abundance is out of reach. But that's not the truth.

That's theft.

Jesus came to reverse the robbery. To restore what was lost. To return what was stolen.

Liberation doesn't always look like a dramatic escape. Sometimes it's the quiet realization that you don't have to stay bound to fear, shame, guilt, or the expectations of others. Jesus came to give you more. Not just materially, but mentally, emotionally, spiritually, and relationally.

So today, start here: You were made for more. Not because of what you can do, but because of who God is, and what He promised.

Prayer Starter

Lord, thank You for coming so I can live fully and freely. Help me release the limitations I've accepted and embrace the abundant life You promised. Show me where I've allowed the enemy to steal my joy or distort my view of You. Teach me to trust Your version of freedom and to live with expectancy instead of fear.

Journal Prompt

Where in your life have you been settling for less than God's promise? What would living an "abundant life" look like for you today?

DAY 2
Never First, Always Second

Scripture: Galatians 4:6–7 (Common English Bible, CEB)

"Because you are sons and daughters, God sent the Spirit of his Son into our hearts, crying, "Abba, Father!" Therefore, you are no longer a slave but a son or daughter, and if you are his child, then you are also an heir through God."

Reflection

Have you ever felt like you were invited as the "plus one" to your own life - present, but not the one the invitation was really meant for? Like everyone else has received a special invitation and place card with their name on it and you didn't. It feels like you were invited only as a second best or last resort to fill an unreserved seat not because you were first choice or intended to be in the room.

Excited for the invitation, you show up, grateful to be there, yet quietly have convinced yourself you didn't really need to be properly celebrated or acknowledged by name. Many of us carry that second-place mindset into our relationships, our work, and even our faith. We settle with being tolerated, not chosen. Accepted, but not fully embraced. We serve in God's house but struggle to believe we belong at His table. And the lie is subtle but powerful: this is your place in the room, where you are allowed to be here - just not fully.

That's the lie.

Belonging was never meant to be earned; it was always meant to be received.

The truth is: you are not a second thought. You are a first-choice child of God.

The enemy's strategy is subtle. He doesn't always attack your talent or your appearance. He goes after your identity. If he can get you to doubt your identity, he can distract you from your calling. But Galatians reminds us: we're not outsiders looking in. We're sons. We're daughters. We're heirs. We have access not because of what we've done, but because of who we belong to.

Liberation begins when you stop trying to earn what's already yours.

Prayer Starter

God, I've spent too much time living like an outsider, afraid to take up space, unsure of my place in Your heart. But today, I choose truth over lies. Remind me that I am Yours. Help me live like a loved child, not a tolerated servant. Teach me to walk boldly in my inheritance as Your heir.

Journal Prompt

Where in your life have you felt like a second-class citizen—even with God? What might change if you believed, deep down, that you are fully accepted, loved, and chosen?

DAY 3
Grace Over Grind

Scripture: Ephesians 2:8–9 (NIV)

"For it is by grace you have been saved, through faith—and this is not from yourselves, it is the gift of God— not by works, so that no one can boast."

Reflection

We live in a world that rewards hustle. Prove yourself. Earn your place. Work for love. And if you're not exhausted, you are not trying hard enough. That mindset doesn't just show up in careers, it creeps into our spirituality. We start to believe we have to perform to earn God's love too. That we have to be "good enough" to deserve His grace.

But grace with God was never about earning.

Ephesians reminds us that salvation, our rescue, our redemption, and our restored identity comes by grace alone. Not effort. Not merit. Not reputation. Grace is unearned. Undeserved. And completely ours through faith in Jesus Christ.

The enemy wants you to believe you must strive for what God already gave you. That if you just do more, serve more, give more, then maybe, just maybe, you'll be enough. But that's not freedom. That's slavery in a spiritual disguise. Slavery is bondage disguised as obligation - where your freedom is restricted, and your worth is tied to your output. It is the quiet belief that you must work to earn what was already given, striving under pressure instead of resting in promise.

Liberation means choosing grace over grind. It means resting in the truth that you are already loved, already chosen, already accepted. Not because you proved your worth, but because Jesus declared it.

Prayer Starter

God, I've spent too long trying to earn what You freely gave. Forgive me for believing the lie that I have to perform to be loved by you and others. Teach me to rest in Your grace. Help me receive Your gift without shame or striving. Remind me that Your approval is not based on my works, but on Your love.

Journal Prompt

Where in your life are you still trying to earn love, approval, or acceptance? How would your thoughts and actions shift if you believed, certainly, that you're already enough by God's grace?

DAY 4
Not Validated, Chosen

Scripture: John 15:16 (NIV)

"You did not choose me, but I chose you and appointed you so that you might go and bear fruit—fruit that will last..."

Reflection

Have you ever found yourself waiting for someone else to see your value before you moved forward? A mentor to endorse you. A friend to confirm you. A room to applaud you. If we're honest, many of us have spent years seeking validation from people who were never authorized to approve us. But Jesus makes it plain: "You did not choose me, but I chose you."

You were chosen before you were liked. Appointed before you were affirmed. Selected by God long before anyone clapped for you. And that means your calling doesn't need a consensus.

Freedom begins when you stop waiting for a committee and start trusting your Creator. He saw something in you before you saw it in yourself. And He's not asking for a vote. He's inviting you to bear fruit, lasting, eternal, kingdom-impacting fruit.

Validation is fleeting. But being chosen by God? That's forever.

Let this truth settle into your soul: You are already enough, already equipped, and already appointed for this moment, this mission, this move.

Prayer Starter

God, I've spent too long seeking approval from people who can't see my full worth. But You chose me. You called me. And today, I receive that truth. Help me stop performing for applause and start producing fruit that honors You. Teach me to rest in my chosenness and walk boldly in my purpose.

Journal Prompt

Where in your life have you been waiting for human approval to move forward? What would shift if you believed, without any doubts, that God has already chosen and appointed you?

DAY 5
Embracing My Divine Design

Scripture: Psalm 139:14 (NIV)

"I praise you because I am fearfully and wonderfully made; your works are wonderful, I know that full well."

Reflection

Liberation doesn't just come from knowing you're chosen, it comes from embracing who God created you to be. Too often, we celebrate God's goodness in others while silently rejecting His design and good in ourselves. We compare, diminish, and doubt ourselves, asking why we weren't made with different gifts, a different story, or a different journey.

But Psalm 139 isn't a generic statement. It's a personal declaration. You are fearfully and wonderfully made. Not accidentally. Not inadequately. A perfect creation.

You don't have to strive to become enough, you already are. You were crafted by the Creator with divine intentionality. Every part of your being, personality, experiences, quirks, and voice were all designed on purpose, for purpose.

God doesn't create fillers. He creates vessels.

So today, the invitation is this: embrace your divine design. Not just in theory—but in how you speak to yourself, how you make decisions, how you carry your calling. Stop waiting to be more polished before you praise God for how He made you. Worship Him now, because you are His wonderful masterpiece.

Prayer Starter

God, I confess that I haven't always seen myself through Your eyes. I've compared, criticized, and questioned who I am or why me. But today, I choose to believe what You say. I am fearfully and wonderfully made. Help me embrace my divine design and walk confidently in who You created me to be.

Journal Prompt

Where have you rejected parts of yourself that God intentionally created? What would it look like to live as someone who believes they are fearfully and wonderfully made?

DAY 6
Obedience Over Certainty

Scripture: 1 Samuel 15:22 (NIV)

"But Samuel replied: 'Does the Lord delight in burnt offerings and sacrifices as much as in obeying the Lord? To obey is better than sacrifice, and to heed is better than the fat of rams."

Reflection

We often ask God for details: What will happen? When will it happen? Will it work out? But sometimes God offers only a whisper, a nudge, a name. He doesn't always give clarity. He gives an opportunity for obedience.

The world teaches us to wait for certainty; to weigh the risks, calculate the outcomes, and only move when everything is secure. But Kingdom living requires a different posture: trusting God more than the plan. Moving when He says go, even when you can't see the whole map.

Obedience doesn't always feel safe. It can be awkward, inconvenient, and unclear. But it is always blessed. Because obedience is worship. It's saying: *God, I trust You more than I trust myself, my thoughts, my strategy, my plans.* I believe that what You see is greater than what I understand.

You don't have to know all the answers to obey. You just need a yes. A willing heart. And the faith to believe that even when it doesn't make sense, God is working something far beyond what you can see.

Prayer Starter

God, I confess that I sometimes crave clarity more than communion. I want answers instead of intimacy. But today, I choose obedience over certainty. Teach me to trust Your timing, respond to Your nudges, and walk by faith, even when the path is unclear.

Journal Prompt

Where in your life is God asking for obedience before explanation? What's one area where you can respond with a faithful "yes" today?

DAY 7
Worth The Wait

Scripture: Isaiah 40:31 (New King James Version, NKJV)

"But those who wait on the Lord shall renew their strength;
They shall mount up with wings like eagles,
They shall run and not be weary,
They shall walk and not faint."

Reflection

Waiting is rarely comfortable. It stretches our patience, tests our faith, and reveals our idols. But Scripture doesn't just tell us to wait, it shows us how. "Those who wait on the Lord" aren't passive. They are anchored. Rooted in trust. Positioned for renewal.

There's a kind of strength that only comes in waiting. Not the kind that flexes in public, but the kind that holds you steady in private. The kind that lifts your head when your heart is tired. The kind that helps you walk forward, even when the answer hasn't come yet.

God isn't late. He's aligning. Preparing. Strengthening. And while you wait, He is not silent. He is renewing you from the inside out, your perspective, your energy, your confidence, your hope.

This verse reminds us: those who wait *on the Lord*, not on outcomes, not on timelines, will be lifted. Carried. Empowered. Waiting isn't punishment. It's preparation for flight.

Prayer Starter

God, I confess waiting is hard. It makes me question, doubt, and sometimes want to give up. But today, I choose to wait on You, not the outcome. Renew my strength. Lift my heart. Anchor me in Your presence. Teach me to trust that Your timing is perfect and that my hope in You is never wasted.

Journal Prompt

What are you waiting for in this season? How might God be using this waiting time to strengthen or prepare you?

DAY 8
Trusting God in Transition

Scripture: Proverbs 3:5–6 (NIV)

"Trust in the Lord with all your heart and lean not on your own understanding; in all your ways submit to him, and he will make your paths straight."

Reflection

Transitions can be holy ground or heartache, sometimes both. Whether it's a career shift, a move, a relationship or friendship change, or something more internal, transitions have a way of surfacing our desire for control. We want guarantees. Safety. Comfort. Certainty. Clarity. But God often invites us to walk before we see.

It's in these in-between spaces that trust is truly tested. We say we believe, but transitions reveal whether our faith is in God's plan or our own. Proverbs 3 doesn't promise we'll always understand the process, it promises we'll be guided. Not by what we see, but by who He is.

It's saying, "God, I don't know what's next, but I know You. And You know all things from the beginning of time until the end of creation. I don't know where this leads, but I trust that You've gone before me and that I'm walking the path You have laid out."

Trusting God in transition doesn't mean you won't feel fear. It means fear doesn't get the final word. It means you keep moving even if all you have is a whisper and a promise. Because His track record is undefeated. In the black church we say, He's never failed you yet.

Prayer Starter

God, I'm in a space that feels uncertain. Help me to release my need to understand and lean into faith. Remind me that Your plan is better than mine, and Your path is trustworthy even when it's unclear. I submit my next steps to You. Direct my path and give me peace as I move forward.

Journal Prompt

Where are you currently navigating a transition? How might God be inviting you to trust Him more deeply in this space of uncertainty?

DAY 9
Released and Restored

Scripture: Isaiah 43:18–19 (NIV)

"Forget the former things; do not dwell on the past. See, I am doing a new thing! Now it springs up; do you not perceive it?"

Reflection

Some things feel unforgettable, what they did, what you lost, what you endured. And yet, God invites you to forget, not because it didn't matter, but because it no longer defines you. You are not what happened. You are what's being healed.

Isaiah 43 reminds us that restoration is God's specialty. But to receive it, you must release what no longer serves your future. You can't hold onto the ashes and expect to carry the oil. You can't keep rehearsing old pain and expect new peace to bloom.

Lot's wife looked back and turned to salt. Not because she made a quick glance, but because her heart was still tethered to what God had already called her out of. Looking back is tempting. But liberation quires forward vision.

God is doing a new thi in you. But the question is whether He's moving the qu tion is whether you'll perce it. Will you see it? Will y make room for it? Will you lease what's behind so you c embrace what's ahead?

You are not bound to yc past. You are being restored His grace. Let Him do the n thing, starting today.

Prayer Starter

God, I confess that I've held on to things You asked me to release. Help me to trust that what's ahead is greater than what's behind. Heal the places in me that are still looking back. I want to perceive the new thing You are doing in my life. Restore me as I release what no longer belongs to me.

Journal Prompt

What are you still carrying from the past that may be blocking your ability to perceive what God is doing now? If nothing comes to mind right away, consider this: Are there intrusive thoughts or memories that surface, even when you don't want to focus on them? What would it look like to truly let those things go?

DAY 10
Forgiveness Is An Act of Faith

Scripture: Luke 17:3–4 (NIV)

"So watch yourselves. If your brother or sister sins against you, rebuke them; and if they repent, forgive them. Even if they sin against you seven times in a day and seven times come back to you saying 'I repent,' you must forgive them."

Colossians 3:13 (NIV)

"Bear with each other and forgive one another if any of you has a grievance against someone. Forgive as the Lord forgave you."

Reflection

Forgiveness does not always feel holy. Sometimes, it feels like loss. Like surrender. Like letting someone get away with what they should be held accountable for. But scripture is clear: forgiveness isn't based on your feelings—it's based on your faith.

Jesus said that if someone sins against you, even seven times in one day, and they repent, you must forgive them. That's not natural. That's not easy. That's spiritual obedience. It's an act of faith.

Faith that God sees what you endured.

Faith that justice doesn't disappear when you forgive.

Faith that healing can happen without an apology.

Faith that you are releasing the weight, not excusing the harm.

And Paul reminds us in Colossians that forgiveness isn't just about them. It's about remembering how much you've been forgiven. Grace is never one-way. God extends it to you so you can extend it to others—not from obligation, but from overflow.

Forgiveness is a process, not a pass.

It's a choice, not a feeling.

And sometimes, it's an act of faith you have to make over and over until your heart catches up with your obedience.

Whether the offense is fresh or decades old, whether it's been acknowledged or not, God invites you to let Him handle the justice so you can receive the peace. The act of forgiveness is an act of freedom. And every time you choose it, you're choosing to walk lighter, live freer, and heal deeper.

Prayer Starter

God, forgiveness is hard. I confess that there are people and situations I'm still holding in my heart, some out of pain, others out of fear. But today, I choose obedience over bitterness. I release the need to keep score and ask You to help me forgive as You forgive me, fully, freely, and repeatedly. Make forgiveness a practice in my life.

Journal Prompt

Who in your life have you struggled to forgive? What would it look like to hand that person or situation over to God? Is there an area where you need to forgive yourself?

DAY 11
The Holy Cadence of Rest

Scripture: Matthew 11:28–30 (The Message Bible, MSG)

"Are you tired? Worn out? Burned out on religion? Come to me. Get away with me, and you'll recover your life. I'll show you how to take a real rest. Walk with me and work with me—watch how I do it. Learn the unforced rhythms of grace. I won't lay anything heavy or ill-fitting on you. Keep company with me, and you'll learn to live freely and lightly."

Reflection

Jesus didn't only model how to work. He modeled how to rest. He withdrew from the crowds, left needs unmet, and made space to commune with the Father— even when people were still waiting to be healed, taught, or helped. He showed us that boundaries aren't barriers to purpose, they're part of it.

But for many of us, rest feels foreign. We've been taught that productivity equals worth. That slowing down is selfish. That rest must be earned. So we keep pushing, pouring, performing—until there's nothing left. And then we wonder why we feel spiritually dry, emotionally brittle, or physically exhausted.

Jesus invites us to something better: rhythm. Not hustle. Not depletion. But a divine cadence of work and rest, of purpose and pause. He doesn't demand that we fix everything before coming to Him. He simply says, "Come. Release. Rest."

Rest isn't just a nap or a vacation. It's a posture. A decision to trust God more than your own effort. To believe that He's still working even when you're not. That your value isn't in your output but in your identity.

What if rest isn't weakness but wisdom? What if real strength is found in your willingness to pause and receive?

Today, Jesus isn't asking you to do more. He's inviting you to do less with Him.

Prayer Starter

Jesus, I'm tired. I've carried burdens You never asked me to hold. Teach me the unforced rhythms of grace. Show me how to walk with You, not just work for You. Help me release the guilt around rest and receive it as a gift. I want to live freely and lightly in step with You.

Journal Prompt

Where in your life have you been resisting rest? What would it look like to embrace the rhythm of rest as a spiritual act of trust?

DAY 12
Chosen to Break the Pattern

Scripture: Esther 4:14 (NIV)

"And who knows but that you have come to your royal position for such a time as this?"

Scripture: Deuteronomy 30:19 (NIV)

"This day I call the heavens and the earth as witnesses against you that I have set before you life and death, blessings and curses. Now choose life, so that you and your children may live."

Reflection

Some inheritances aren't handed down, they're handed back. Cycles of silence. Echoes of fear. Patterns of pain passed from one generation to the next like a worn-out story begging for a new ending.

And then God speaks: You are the new chapter.

Esther's courage didn't just rescue her people. It rerouted a legacy. She wasn't qualified by status or strength; she was positioned by purpose. At the hinge of history, she stood in a palace and decided: This ends with me. Freedom begins here.

You may not wear a crown, but heaven sees your "yes" the same way. When you choose healing over hiding, truth over silence, presence over performance, you rewrite what's possible. You choose life. Not just for you, but for those who follow.

This is what it means to be chosen: Not simply to be blessed, but to become the blessing. To rise, although generations before you fell. To build what they never saw. To believe that God's promise includes you—and everyone tied to your name.

So, stand in your yes today. The ripple is already forming.

Prayer Starter

God, thank You for calling me to more. I choose life today, not just for myself, but for those coming after me. Make me bold like Esther. Let my obedience break patterns and plant blessings. I trust You with the future You're shaping through me.

Journal Prompt

What does it mean to you to be a pattern-breaker? Where do you feel God calling you to choose a new way forward for your sake and for future generations?

DAY 13
Divinely Drafted

"You did not choose me, but I chose you and appointed you so that you might go and bear fruit—fruit that will last..."

Reflection

In every sports draft, there's a number one pick. A standout. A player so valuable that teams compete to get them. And guess what? In heaven's draft, you were God's top choice.

He wasn't scrambling to fill a roster. He wasn't choosing based on popularity, pedigree, or stats. He picked you because He wanted you. He wanted you to play, not to sit on the bench. He created you to lead. To bear fruit that lasts.

You didn't audition for this. You didn't have to sell yourself or convince God you were worthy. Before you ever stepped onto the field of life, He had already called your name. You've been divinely drafted and hand-selected for a divine assignment.

And like any top draft pick, you'll be stretched. The training is real. The expectations may feel high. But so is the potential. God equips those He calls. And His playbook? It always leads to victory, even when the plays feel unfamiliar.

So no more waiting for permission. No more questioning if you belong in the game. You're not just on the team—you're in the game, carrying purpose, power, and divine strategy.

You weren't a fallback. You're not a walk-on. You are a first-round draft pick, God's choice!

Prayer Starter

God, thank You for choosing me, not as an afterthought, but as Your first pick. Help me step fully into the assignment You've given me. When I feel unqualified, remind me that You called me anyway. I trust Your process, Your playbook, and Your power working through and in me.

Journal Prompt

What does it mean to you that God chose you first, fully, and on purpose? Where have you been holding back like a benchwarmer when God has already put you in the game?

DAY 14
Fully Known, Fully Loved

Scripture: Romans 8:38–39 (NIV)

"For I am convinced that neither death nor life, neither angels nor demons, neither the present nor the future, nor any powers, neither height nor depth, nor anything else in all creation, will be able to separate us from the love of God that is in Christ Jesus our Lord."

Scripture: Joshua 1:9 (NIV)

"Have I not commanded you? Be strong and courageous. Do not be afraid; do not be discouraged, for the Lord your God will be with you wherever you go."

Reflection

There is no part of you hidden from God. He sees all your fears, failures, dreams, and contradictions, yet He stays. That kind of love is rare. And when you fully accept that you are fully known and fully loved by the One who made you, something shifts. You stop performing. You stop pretending. And you start showing up boldly as the person God designed you to be.

Romans 8 assures us that nothing can separate us from God's love. Not our past. Not our mistakes. Not our insecurities. Not the things we're still working through. His love is not earned—it's extended. Constant. Unshakable. And when that truth settles deep into your heart, it gives birth to holy confidence.

Confidence isn't arrogance. It's alignment. It's walking with the quiet knowing that God is with you and that His love equips you to stand firm, speak truth, and move forward even when you feel unqualified. It's the courage to obey without having all the answers. To testify without fear of judgment. To walk boldly in your divine assignment even when others don't understand it.

Joshua was called to lead without a blueprint, but God's command was clear: Be strong and courageous… I am with you. That same command is yours. You don't have to shrink. You don't

have to second-guess your are also fully empowered.
worth. When you are rooted
in God's love, you can rise in
His strength.

When you are fully
known and fully loved, you

Prayer Starter

God, thank You for knowing me completely and loving
me unconditionally. Your love gives me the courage to show
up as my full self. Help me to trust Your voice above all
others and to walk confidently in my purpose. Teach me to
live boldly, love deeply, and obey quickly knowing You are
always with me.

Journal Prompt

What would change if you believed, deep in your bones, that you are fully known and fully loved by God? How might your confidence, decisions, or testimony shift if you stopped hiding and started walking boldly in that truth?

DAY 15
No Longer Negotiating My Worth

Scripture: Galatians 1:10 (NIV)

"Am I now trying to win the approval of human beings, or of God? Or am I trying to please people? If I were still trying to please people, I would not be a servant of Christ."

Reflection

There comes a point when you stop shrinking to fit spaces God never assigned you to. When you stop over-explaining, over-functioning, and over-apologizing just to be accepted. When you stop asking, "Do they see my value?" and start declaring, "I know who I am."

That point is liberation.

For years, you may have negotiated your worth by toning down your brilliance, staying silent to keep the peace, or saying yes when you wanted or needed to say no. Not because you lacked value, but because you weren't yet convinced you were allowed to own it.

But something has shifted. You've changed your habits. You've learned your rhythm. You've stopped waiting for external validation to confirm what God has already said.

Galatians 1:10 reminds us: people-pleasing and divine purpose don't mix. If your goal is to be liked by everyone, you will constantly abandon yourself. But when your aim is to serve God—fully, faithfully, and freely—you will no longer need to edit your authenticity.

You are not a bargain. You are not a backup plan. You are God's workmanship, worthy of rooms you didn't campaign for and callings you didn't create. Your worth is not up for negotiation. It is sealed by the One who called you by name.

Prayer Starter

God, thank You for affirming my identity. I no longer need to shrink, perform, or explain myself to be worthy. Help me release the need for approval and walk in alignment with who You say I am. Teach me to serve You above all else, and to never compromise my calling for comfort.

Journal Prompt

Where have you been negotiating your worth or seeking permission to be who God already called you to be? What would it look like to fully own your identity? What would be different?

DAY 16
The Power of a Sacred No

Scripture: Ecclesiastes 3:1, 5 (NIV)

"There is a time for everything... a time to embrace and a time to refrain from embracing."

Scripture: Matthew 5:37 (NIV)

"All you need to say is simply 'Yes' or 'No' anything beyond this comes from the evil one."

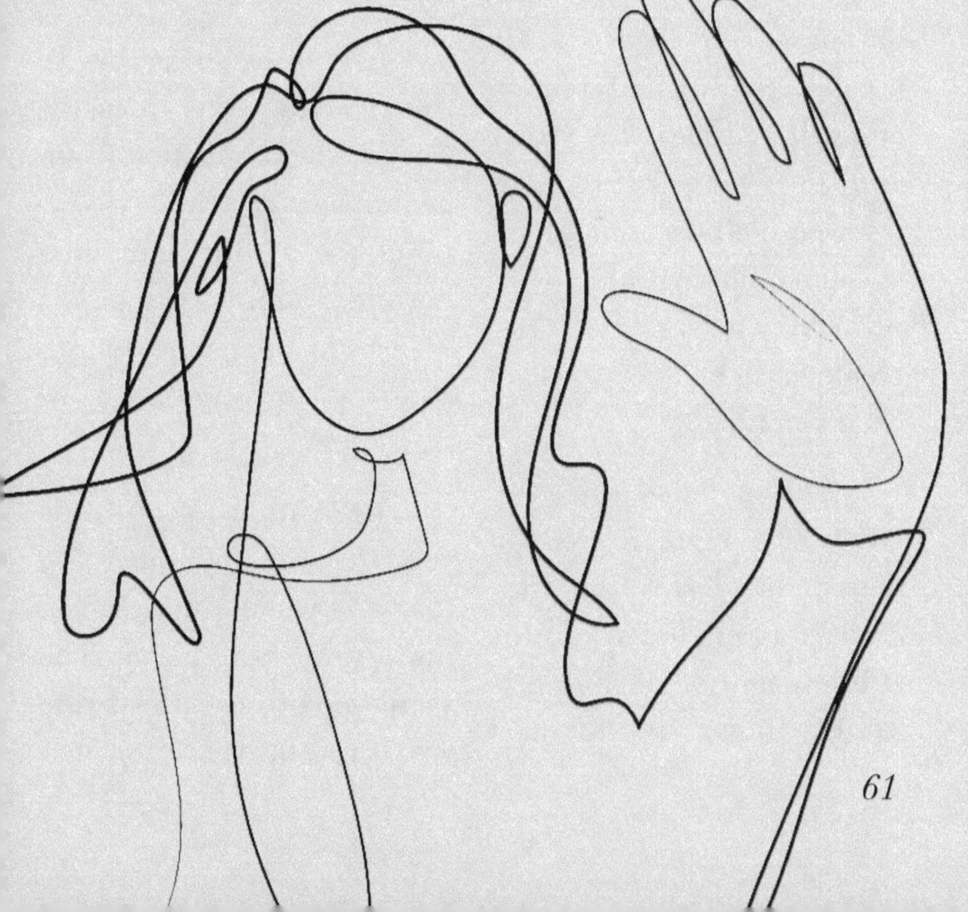

Reflection

We often celebrate the divine "yes," the open door, the new assignment, the leap of faith. But there's another kind of obedience that's just as holy: the sacred no.

From the very beginning, God established boundaries. He separated light from darkness, land from sea. He created rhythm in creation allocating times for work and times for rest. Boundaries weren't born out of restriction, but wisdom. They preserve what's sacred. They create order. They protect what's holy.

Jesus modeled this with clarity. Though He was in high demand, He often withdrew to pray. He left crowds at the height of His popularity. He didn't stay to meet every need or answer every request. Not because He lacked compassion but because He was committed to His assignment.

There is power in knowing when to refrain, when to step away, and when to say no without guilt.

Many of us struggle with this. We say yes to preserve relationships, maintain appearances, or avoid disappointment. But anything beyond a simple yes or no, Jesus said, opens the door to confusion, manipulation, or fear.

The truth is: every time you say yes to something that isn't yours, you're saying no to something that is. The sacred no protects the divine yes. It creates space for obedience, clarity, and peace.

Your "no" doesn't need justification. It doesn't need to be softened with over-explaining or spiritual guilt. If Jesus, the Savior of the world, said no to good things to preserve God's things, so can you.

And when you do, you're not being rude. You're being reverent.

Prayer Starter

God, thank You for showing me that boundaries are holy. Give me the courage to say "no" when I need to, and the wisdom to know when a "yes" would cost me too much. Teach me to follow Your rhythm—not the demands of others. Help me to protect the space where You dwell and to honor my divine assignment with clarity and conviction.

Journal Prompt

Where have you been saying yes out of guilt or obligation? What would it look like to embrace the sacred no, knowing that it protects your peace, purpose, and obedience to God?

DAY 17
Joy Is My Rebellion

Scripture: Romans 15:13 (NIV))

"May the God of hope fill you with all joy and peace as you trust in him, so that you may overflow with hope by the power of the Holy Spirit."

Reflection

Joy isn't a personality trait. It's not a byproduct of easy days. Joy is a weapon; one the enemy hopes you never pick up.

When you've been through trauma, disappointment, or deep grief, the world starts expecting your dimming. People wait for you to crumble. But joy? Joy throws them off. It says, "You don't get to define me by what I've been through. My story is still being written."

That's why choosing joy is rebellious. It disrupts despair. It breaks the rhythm of resignation. It's not about pretending everything is okay; it's about declaring that even if it's not, God still is. Joy is the sound of heaven in a weary soul.

And here's the truth: joy is holy. It is sacred defiance in a world ruled by negativity, fear, and shame. When you smile after loss, laugh during healing, and celebrate while still becoming, that's warfare. That's worship.

Romans reminds us that joy is not self-produced, it's Spirit-powered. As you trust God, He fills you. As you lean into His hope, you overflow. That means you don't have to force it. You just have to stay open. Stay expectant. Stay anchored in the One who never stops pouring.

Let joy be your rebellion today. Let it be your declaration that your story isn't over, and it's going to end in glory.

Prayer Starter

God of hope, fill me again. I don't want to fake joy; I want to receive it. Remind me that joy is my inheritance, not a luxury. Help me resist the heaviness that tries to settle on my spirit. I trust You to restore my strength through joy. I choose to overflow, even here.

Journal Prompt

Where in your life does joy feel hard to access? What would it look like to reclaim joy as a form of spiritual resistance instead of emotional denial?

DAY 18
Grief Is Holy Too

Scripture: Psalm 34:18 (NIV)

"The Lord is close to the brokenhearted and saves those who are crushed in spirit."

Scripture: Luke 22:42 (NIV)

"Father, if you are willing, take this cup from me; yet not my will, but yours be done."

Reflection

We don't always talk about grief as spiritual practice. We rush through it. Bury it. Quote scriptures over it. But the truth is: grief is holy too.

Jesus, fully divine and fully human, felt the weight of sorrow so deeply that He wept at a friend's Lazarus' tomb and cried out to his Father, Abba, in Garden of Gethsemane. He didn't bypass His emotions to prove His strength. He surrendered them. And in doing so, He showed us what true liberation looks like. It looks like honesty not denial. It looks like trust, not control.

There are things you've lost that deserve to be grieved. Dreams. Relationships. Seasons of life that didn't turn out the way you hoped. Liberation doesn't mean pretending those things didn't happen or have meaning to you. It means letting God hold your heart while you name them, mourn them, and slowly release them.

Psalm 34 reminds us: God is near. Not just when we're praising Him but also when we're crushed. When we can barely pray. When the tears won't stop. He doesn't rush us through our sadness. He sits in it with us. Present. Tender. Unmoving.

And like Jesus in the garden, you can ask for the cup to pass. You can be honest about your pain. You can say, "This hurts. I didn't want this." And then, when you're ready, you can say,

"But I trust You anyway."

Grief is not the absence of faith. It's part of the walk. And God calls even that part sacred. Examples of this are when Hannah and her grief of not having a child, crying out in faith to God; Jesus crying at the loss of Lazarus in grief yet holding tight to his faith; Jesus crying at the thought of going through the pain of losing his human life yet saying not my will but yours.

Prayer Starter

Lord, thank You for staying close when my heart is broken. Help me to stop pretending that I'm okay when I'm not. Teach me how to grieve in Your presence with honesty, trust, and surrender. I give You what hurts, and I ask You to hold it gently.

Journal Prompt

What losses have you been carrying in silence? What would it look like to grieve them honestly with God, not apart from Him?

DAY 19
Becoming Whole, Not Flawless

Scripture: Philippians 1:6 (NIV)

"...being confident of this, that he who began a good work in you will carry it on to completion until the day of Christ Jesus."

Reflection

Wholeness is not the absence of flaws; it's the presence of grace.

We often confuse healing with perfection, thinking we have to get it all right before we can walk boldly in purpose. But God doesn't wait for flawless vessels to do mighty things. He uses willing ones. And wholeness, in His eyes, is about alignment, not achievement.

Philippians reminds us that the good work God began in you is still unfolding. He's not in a rush. He's not surprised by your stumbles. And He's certainly not comparing your progress to anyone else's. Your journey is sacred, even when it's messy.

You are becoming whole every time you choose truth over denial. Every time you forgive yourself or someone else. Every time you show up when it would be easier to shrink. That's the work. That's the progress. That's the grace.

Perfection isn't the goal. Presence is. Progress is. And the God who started the work in you? He's not letting go until it's complete.

So take a deep breath. You're not behind. You're not broken. You're becoming.

Prayer Starter

God, thank You that I don't have to be flawless to be loved or used by You. Help me to release the pressure to be perfect and rest in the truth that I'm a work in progress. Remind me that wholeness includes grace, growth, and gentle transformation. I trust You to finish what You started in me.

Journal Prompt

Where have you been placing pressure on yourself to be perfect? If a friend were applying pressure to be perfect upon themselves, what kind of tangible advice would you offer them? What is preventing you from practicing that advice? How might you begin to accept that God is not finished with you yet?

DAY 20
Walking in the Light

Scripture: Matthew 5:14–16 (NIV)

"You are the light of the world. A town built on a hill cannot be hidden. Neither do people light a lamp and put it under a bowl. Instead, they put it on its stand, and it gives light to everyone in the house. In the same way, let your light shine before others, that they may see your good deeds and glorify your Father in heaven."

Reflection

You were never meant to hide.

Not your story.

Not your healing.

Not your light.

After everything you've walked through, every lie you've released, every wound you've surrendered, every truth you've reclaimed, you are not the same. And now, it's time to live like it. Boldly. Freely. Publicly. As a light.

Jesus didn't call you the hopeful of the world. He didn't say, "Someday you'll be the light." He said you are the light. Right now. Even with your imperfections, your past, your questions, your light is needed. And not for your glory, but for His.

You don't have to manufacture brightness. The Light lives in you. Your job isn't to shine perfectly; it's to shine authentically. When you live in truth, you illuminate freedom. When you walk in alignment, you offer a path for others to follow. This is not about performance. It's about presence. God's presence in you, reflected through you.

And make no mistake: Light disrupts darkness. So don't be surprised when your healing unsettles those still hiding. Don't dim your testimony to make others comfortable. Don't hide your boldness under the weight of someone else's expectations. You were placed on that hill on purpose. Not to be seen for your sake, but to help others see Him.

Prayer Starter

God, thank You for calling me to be light in a world that often feels dim. Help me walk in truth, shine in love, and live in alignment with You. Give me the courage to be visible—not for applause, but for impact. Let my life reflect Your glory, one step at a time.

Journal Prompt

Where have you wrestled with dimming your light to fit in or stay comfortable? What would it look like to live fully lit, open, honest, and aligned with who God created you to be?

DAY 21
Living Liberated

Scripture: Matthew 10:7–8 (NKJV)

"And as you go, preach, saying, 'The kingdom of heaven is at hand.' Heal the sick, cleanse the lepers, raise the dead, cast out demons. Freely you have received, freely give."

Scripture: John 14:12 (NKJV)

"Most assuredly, I say to you, he who believes in Me, the works that I do he will do also; and greater works than these he will do, because I go to My Father."

Reflection

Liberation is not just a feeling. It's a calling. A commissioning. A divine reminder that your healing was never meant to stop with you. You were set free so you could set others free.

Jesus invited us to watch Him work miracles, and He empowered us to continue His work. Through His death and resurrection, and with the gift of the Holy Spirit, we have been given access to the same power that raised Him from the grave. That power lives in you.

You are no longer bound.

You are no longer silenced.

You are no longer waiting to be chosen.

You have been called to proclaim, to heal, to deliver, and to give freely what God has poured so generously into you.

This is what it means to live liberated:

To walk boldly into dark places and bring light.

To speak truth with love and authority.

To break generational chains with prayer, presence, and power.

To do greater things, not for your glory, but for His.

You are God's vessel. His ambassador. His light-bearer.

So as you go into your workplace, your family, your community remember what you carry.

You're not just a recipient of freedom, you're a carrier of it.

You don't walk away from this journey empty-handed.

You carry a torch.

Not a fragile flame, but a fire lit by the All-Consuming God. The One who heals, restores, illuminates, and ignites.

Jesus didn't just die to set you free. He rose so you could rise too.

And because of Him, you've been equipped to go into the world. To heal the sick. To raise the dead. To cast out darkness.

Freely you have received. Freely give.

Prayer Starter

God, thank You for setting me free and for entrusting me with power and purpose. Help me to walk in Your authority with humility, boldness, and love. Remind me daily that the same Spirit that raised Jesus lives in me. I want to do greater things, not for applause, but for Your glory. Use me to bring light wherever You send me.

Journal Prompt

Where do you feel God calling you to carry the light of liberation? What "greater thing" feels impossible but might just be your next assignment?

About Me

Syrena N. Williams

I am first and foremost a child of God, and someone who believes deeply in the power and responsibility of relationships. I am a mother, daughter, sister, cousin, and a true friend. This is how I move through the world. I value presence, honesty, compassion, and the quiet work of truly knowing and caring for the people in my life. I am drawn to relationships that are meaningful and rooted in genuine care.

Like many people, I grew up surrounded by expectations, opinions, and narratives about who I should be and how I should move through the world. Some of those voices attempted to shape how I presented myself, while others used words that quietly chipped away at my confidence and self-esteem. Over time, I began to believe many of those messages as my truth.

Through God's continual tugging, reflection, faith, and life experience, I began to recognize that those narratives did not define me. Instead, I continued becoming who God was transforming me into.

One of the prayers that continues to shape my life is God allow me to see You in myself and in the people around me. When I approach others through that lens, everything shifts. It invites me to look beyond labels, assumptions, and past narratives and to recognize people as God sees them.

I understand that part of my role in the lives of others is simply to serve as a mirror, helping them recognize themselves as wonderfully made.

For many years, my work has involved walking alongside individuals and organizations as they learn, grow, and build meaningful lives and work. Along the way, my professional roles have included serving as an attorney, business consultant, coach, and educator. As my perspective deepened, the way I engaged my work began to change. Walking alongside people moved from being a task to becoming an honor. Development became less about solutions and more about caring for the whole person. Those relationships often grow into thought partnerships, building sessions, and, at times, discipleship.

Today, much of my work centers around an invitation I extend to others: to live liberated. Living Liberated encourages us to pause and examine the narratives that shape how we see ourselves, what we believe about our worth, and how we move through the world. It is an invitation to release what no longer aligns with truth and to embrace the person God is continually forming us to be.

Through my writing, speaking, and conversations with others, I invite people into the process of reflection and renewal. My book *Living Liberated: Letting Go of the Lies, Labels, and Longing to Be Free,* alongside its devotional companion, creates space for readers to wrestle honestly with their stories while rediscovering identity, freedom, and faith.

When I am not writing, speaking, or journeying with others, you can find me cooking, at the beach, dancing, laughing, and sharing meaningful conversations. There is nothing I enjoy more than building community and creating spaces where people can gather, be themselves, and encourage one another along the way.

Let's Connect